GENERAL SERIES 105

JOHN S. MACAULEY

The Oxford Movement and Anglican Ritualism

NIGEL YATES

The Historical Association,
59a Kennington Park Road, London SE11 4JH

ACKNOWLEDGEMENTS

The picture on the outside front cover is of the altar screen or reredos in Hereford Cathedral designed by J.N. Cottingham as part of his restoration of Hereford Cathedral between 1841 and 1852. The altar has been raised on a footpace and vested in a manner approved of by the ecclesiologists with an embroidered frontal, elaborately bound service books and two candlesticks with tall tapers which appear to be lighted. The picture was published orginally in *Handbook to the Cathedrals of England: Western Division*, 1864 and is reproduced by kind permision of the publisher, John Murrary Limited, London.

The Publication of a pamphlet by the Historical Association does not necessarily imply the Association's official approbation of the opinions expressed therein.

© Nigel Yates, 1983

ISBN 085 278 255 1

HA 8.5/2/83

Printed in Great Britain by The Chameleon Press Ltd, 5-25 Burr Road, Wandsworth, London SW18 4SG

Contents

The Background to the Oxford Movement, *page 5*

Oxford Theology and Cambridge Architecture, *page 11*

Retrospect: The Significance of 1845, *page 21*

The Growth of Ritualism, *page 24*

The Oxford Movement in Perspective, *page 36*

Footnotes, *page 42*

Bibliography, *page 44*

The Background to the Oxford Movement

The High Church Tradition

The English Reformation of the sixteenth century had been a compromise, both politically and theologically. The administrative framework of the medieval church, with its system of church courts, private patronage, pluralism, the social and financial gulf between the lower and higher clergy, its inadequacy of clerical education and its hierarchical structure, had survived virtually intact. The theology of the reformed church's doctrinal standpoint, for instance in the 39 Articles, was, however, basically Calvinist and strongly anti-Roman. Its liturgy managed to incorporate both Protestant and Catholic features. Yet the reformed church won the allegiance, even if grudging, of most English people in the sixteenth century. Only a few remained recusants, loyal to the pope. Only a few extreme Protestants, mostly Anabaptists, could not be accommodated. Yet because the reformed Church of England was a compromise it contained within itself from its earliest days both high and low church pressure groups anxious to push the church in either a more Catholic or a more Protestant direction.

By the early seventeenth century high churchmen had managed to gain the support of the Stuart kings, James I and Charles I. Their defeat along with that of the monarchy in the Civil War of the 1640s was only a temporary setback. With the restoration of Charles II Anglicanism was re-established, the Puritan or low church party was largely driven out of the church into dissenting sects, and the high churchmen who had fled to the Continent in the 1650s were rewarded with bishoprics. The high church triumph was, however, cut short by the abdication and exile of James II in 1688. Many high churchmen who had preached in favour of the divine right of kings and non-resistance to monarchical authority found it impossible to take the oath of allegiance to William

III; more than 400 of them, including the Archbishop of Canterbury and seven other bishops, refused to take the oath and were deprived. Although the non-juring schism only lasted effectively for about forty years it certainly weakened the high church party within Anglicanism. A number of the leading high church writers, such as William Law, were non-jurors. The many high churchmen who did take the oath to William III, and later to the Hanoverians, were to some extent suspected of secret Jacobite sympathies and their influence thereby diminished. The leadership among the bishops passed to those who possessed Erastian views of the relationship between church and state, seeing the former as subservient to the latter even in the matter of religious faith and practice. It was this position which ultimately led to the attempted reform of the church by the state in the 1830s and provoked the conservative religious reaction which was an essential part of the Oxford Movement.

High churchmanship however was far from dead. Throughout the eighteenth century the majority of Anglican clergy remained high church in their attitudes, but it was rather more passive high churchmanship than it had been hitherto. Later critics labelled it, and the prevailing ecclesiastical climate of the eighteenth century, lethargic and undisciplined, but recent research has shown that there was far greater diligence among the clergy than they have previously been given credit for. Indeed the early part of the century was notable for the establishment of religious societies, such as the Societies for Promoting Christian Knowledge (1698) and the Propogation of the Gospel (1701), both nationally and locally. In the late eighteenth century there was a reform movement in several dioceses initiated mostly by high church bishops. It was this prevailing current of conservative high churchmanship which formed the basis of much of the early clerical support for the Oxford Movement in the 1830s.

The Evangelical Revival

The intense conservatism of Anglican high churchmen in the eighteenth century proved rather frustrating to a small number of young high churchmen. In 1729 a group at Oxford, led by John and Charles Wesley, began to meet regularly to pray and to talk about religious matters. They laid great emphasis upon frequent communion, fasting and penitence, all of which they felt were undervalued by their contemporaries, and all of which a century later became hallmarks of the Oxford Movement. They were nicknamed Methodists, because of their 'methodical' attitudes to theological belief and liturgical practice, and they were much distrusted by most Anglican high churchmen for their enthusiasm which was then regarded with great suspicion. In 1738 John Wesley came into contact with the Moravians and underwent a profound spiritual conversion. From that date the Methodists, though many retained high church opinions, moved in a more Evangelical direction. They found that as a result most Anglican pulpits were unavailable to them so they took their message outside the traditional pattern of Anglican worship to open-air meetings for prayer and preaching. John and Charles Wesley had no intention of founding a new denomination. Methodists were a society (they still offically term themselves such) within the Church of England. Towards the end of his life, however, in 1784, John Wesley was persuaded, against his inclinations, to ordain ministers for the strong Methodist following in North America, and this was the first step in the schism which led eventually to the creation of a new denomination. However, in some parts of the country it was well into the nineteenth century before individual members of Methodist societies ceased to regard themselves as Anglicans, worshipping regularly and communicating at the parish church on a Sunday morning, and attending services in their own chapels later in the day.

Not all of those who initially supported the Methodists followed them out of the Church of England. By the middle of the eighteenth century another group of rather more Evangelical clergy and lay people also began to attack the conservatism of the established church and to lay great emphasis on the conversion experience, but they remained within the church, despised and distrusted as much as the Methodists. They took a considerable initiative in missionary work and campaigns for social reform and by the 1820s were beginning to establish a considerable foothold in the parishes, especially in the larger towns where new chapels, managed by trustees and financed from pew-rents, were erected by groups of Evangelicals. By 1830 three Evangelicals had been made bishops. Despite their emphasis on spiritual conversion and the absolute supremacy of Scripture over the traditions of the church, the early Evangelicals were by no means anti-sacramental. Indeed, like the Methodists, they encouraged more frequent communion services, usually celebrated only monthly in most town churches, and often only quarterly in some rural parishes, by conservative churchmen. A number of those brought up as, or influenced by, Evangelicals, in the late eighteenth and early nineteenth centuries, later became participants in or supporters of the Oxford Movement. They did so largely because they had become dissatisfied with the emotionalism within Evangelicalism, and with what they came to regard as the intellectual inadequacy of Evangelical theology. The Oxford Movement was not just a reassertion of traditional Anglican high churchmanship, but it brought together men from different theological, including Evangelical, backgrounds.

Popular Medievalism

The impetus for the Oxford Movement, however, was not purely religious. There were other, less easily defined, anxieties within British society in the early nineteenth century that persuaded many people that essential religious values had to be proclaimed and protected. These anxieties were caused largely by the rapid changes brought about by the shift from a predominantly agricultural and rural society to a predominantly industrial and urban one in the years after 1750. There was a feeling that the traditional order had broken down; that undesirable elements within society, particularly commercially-orientated ones, were taking advantage of that breakdown to further their own interests. The political impact of the French Revolution provoked a strong distrust of political radicalism. People who felt like this, and there were many among the landed and professional classes, sought escape from reality in a sort of romantic medievalism in which the true order of society, with its proper social hierarchy and political stability, was restored and reinforced. This popular medievalism can be seen in much of the literature of the late eighteenth and early nineteenth centuries, notably in the novels and poetry of Sir

Walter Scott and William Wordsworth. It can be seen in the Gothic revival in architecture and sculpture, and particularly in the writings of A.W.N. Pugin; Gothicism began in the late eighteenth century, and it dominated the whole of the nineteenth, and even the early twentieth, centuries. It can be seen politically in the conservatism of the Young England Movement in the 1840s and in the attitudes of the early Christian Socialists. It can be seen artistically in the writings and paintings of the Pre-Raphaelite Brotherhood. It can be seen ecclesiastically in the launching and flourishing of the Oxford Movement.

There were, however, particular ecclesiastical events which prompted and encouraged the Oxford Movement. Pushed by dissenters and radicals, and for most conservative churchmen the two were interchangeable, the government after 1820 began to undertake a wholesale reform of the Church of England, the organisation of which was ill-equipped to deal with the pressures brought about by the changes in society. It began with government support for a programme of building new churches in the populous towns, but it soon moved on to reforms which conservative churchmen found profoundly distasteful. Cathedral Chapters were reformed, sinecures abolished, endownments reallocated. There were even calls from the more radical Whigs for the wholesale reorganisation of the established church as, in effect, a department of government. There was also, in the eyes of conservative churchmen, a conspiracy to destroy the identity of church and state enshrined in the Anglican formularies and in subsequent legislation, with the various measures aimed at placing Anglicans and non-Anglicans on a more equal footing, politically and socially: the repeal of the Test Act and the passing of Catholic Emancipation. Even the Reform Act of 1832, the Poor Law Amendment Act of 1834 and the Municipal Corporations Act of 1835 were interpreted as attacks on the privileges of the established church.

It was in this political and social climate that the Oxford Movement was launched, and it inevitably attracted the support of conservative churchmen, whose interests it was seen to be defending. Initially most high churchmen, including many bishops, and indeed even some Evangelicals, who were also mostly conservatives politically, welcomed a vigorous defence of the Church of England from attacks by dissenters and radicals. It was only when the movement began to be seen as developing Romanising tendencies that many early supporters began to have second thoughts. For however strong the pull of conservatism was, the pull of anti-papalism was a great deal stronger. Eventually these tensions did not just result in the loss of many early supporters from the high church bandwagon, but to serious and bitter divisions among those high churchmen who continued to regard themselves as participants in the Oxford Movement.

Oxford Theology and Cambridge Architecture

The Origins of the Oxford Movement

The origins of the Oxford Movement are to be found in casual discussions within the senior common room at Oriel College, Oxford, in the 1820s. The principal participants were four fellows of the College: John Keble[1], Edward Bouverie Pusey[2], John Henry Newman[3] and Richard Hurrell Froude[4]. Keble, Pusey and Froude were all traditional high churchmen, though there were significant differences between them. Keble was the most conservative, holding a position similar to that of most eighteenth-century high churchmen. Pusey, in the 1820s, was much attracted to German biblical criticism and theological liberalism and was indeed one of the only English theologians of the early nineteenth century not to be substantially insular in his attitudes and experiences; later, however, he took a much more conservative stand and was one of the sternest critics of the English liberal theologians, in particular those who contributed to *Essays and Reviews* in 1860. Froude was an advanced high churchman, one of the very few who were not, like the rest of English society, strongly anti-papalist and who believed that if the Church of England was to truly recover its Catholic heritage then some sort of *rapprochement* with Rome was unavoidable. Unlike the others Newman came from an Evangelical background and had undergone his own conversion experience; however, by the early 1820s he was becoming increasingly dissatisfied with Evangelical theology and was much influenced by his contact with high churchmen, particularly Froude.

In 1827 Keble published *The Christian Year,* a collection of poems for the Sundays and holy days of the year. It became an immediate success, was reprinted throughout the nineteenth century, and provided several hymns for the first edition of *Hymns Ancient and Modern* and most subsequent hymnals. The tone was uncompromisingly Catholic; there was even a hymn to the Virgin Mary beginning 'Ave Maria! Blessed Maid! Lily of Eden's fragrant shade!' Its popularity ensured a ready audience for its author who was invited to preach the assize sermon before the University of Oxford on 14 July 1833, the day which has come to be kept as the official beginning of the Oxford Movement. The Whig government had recently proposed to reduce the number of Irish bishoprics through amalgamation and Keble in his sermon condemned this as an act of national apostasy. As far as the government was concerned this was all part of its general programme of political, social and ecclesiastical reform, noted earlier, to which most high churchmen objected. Keble was simply using the Irish incident as a means of rallying traditional high churchmen to the defence of the Anglican establishment.

Shortly after Keble's sermon a group of high churchmen, including Hurrell Froude, met at Hadleigh Rectory, the home of one of the leading high churchmen outside Oxford, Hugh James Rose[5]; the others present were Arthur Philip Percival[6] and William Palmer[7], who in the previous year had published *Origines Liturgicae*, a learned treatise on the history of the English liturgy. They decided to establish an Association of Friends of the Church, which eventually resulted in an address to the Archbishop of Canterbury signed by a large number of both clergy and laity. The real impact was however made by the decision of the Oxford-based high churchmen to resort to the tactics already familiar in other ecclesiastical, especially Evangelical, circles and to issue a series of tracts.

The Tracts for the Times

The tracts were launched in September 1833 with a four-page leaflet by Newman entitled 'Thoughts on the Ministerial Commission respectfully addressed to the Clergy', a vigorous defence of the doctrine of apostolic succession, as it applied to the Church of England, rather played down by most eighteenth-century bishops. Between 1833 and 1841 a total of ninety tracts were published. Only the first few were short leaflets. They soon developed into substantial pamphlets and some were almost short monographs. Of the ninety tracts, eighteen were selections from the writings of seventeenth or eighteenth century high churchmen, especially Thomas Wilson, Bishop of Sodor and Man from 1698 until 1755. Of the remainder, Newman wrote twenty-six, Pusey wrote seven, including one on fasting and three on baptism, Keble wrote nine, and his brother Thomas four. Other contributors included Froude, Percival, Charles Marriott[8] and Isaac Williams[9]. Williams's tracts on 'Reserve in Communicating Christian Knowledge', in which he argued the need to give cautious expression to high church opinions, for fear of unsettling those who might misunderstand their implications, were regarded by critics as one of the first public examples of Tractarian disloyalty to the Church of England, and cost Williams his deserved election to the Oxford chair of poetry, formerly held by Keble, in 1842.

There is no doubt whatsoever of the widespread influence of the *Tracts for the Times*. The fact that these writers and the other supporters of the Oxford Movement have since been generally termed Tractarians is in itself proof of their effectiveness. They were certainly read by most clergymen and lay people who took an interest, as many did, in theological matters. Among politicians decidedly influenced by the tracts was William Ewart Gladstone, the future prime minister. Significant clerical support for the tracts came from Walter Farquhar Hook[10], Henry Edward Manning[11] and Robert Isaac Wilberforce[12]. There was a good deal of quiet support for the Tractarians from many of the English bishops, most of whom were moderate high churchmen. One outright supporter, however, was Henry Phillpotts, bishop of Exeter from 1830 until 1869. It was only when the tracts appeared to be taking a more extreme high church position that some of this support began to melt away. Indeed at the beginning many of the Evangelicals welcomed a good deal of Tractarian teaching. It was only the liberal broad churchmen who were initially and constantly hostile. The series of tracts was brought to an end suddenly in 1841 with the publication of *Tract XC*, in which Newman sought to put forward the view that the Thirty-Nine Articles, the sixteenth-century doctrinal formulary of the Church of England, were not substantially at variance with official

Roman Catholic teaching but were more criticisms of popular Roman Catholic practices. The tract was considered far too pro-Roman by most Anglicans including many high churchmen, and the controversy which its publication provoked was sufficient to prevent the publication of any further titles in the series.

In assessing the significance of the *Tracts for the Times* it is important to notice three important points. Firstly the tracts were notable for their academic erudition. Only the first few were 'popular' in their presentation. The remainder were works of the highest contemporary scholarship, those of Pusey particularly so. Secondly, it should be noted that the tracts were addressed to the 'clergy'. Although laymen might read them, and certainly many did, they were primarily aimed at the clergy, and there is no doubt that the Tractarian movement, and its later off-shoots, began initially as, and remained substantially, clerically-dominated pressure groups. In this respect they can be contrasted with the various Evangelical groups where there seems to have been a great degree of balance between clerical and non-clerical interests. Thirdly, it is extremely significant that the tracts should have been produced within the University of Oxford. Virtually all future clergymen at that time were educated within the ancient universities of Oxford and Cambridge, particularly the former, as were the sons of the country's leading families. The influence that the tracts wielded therefore was not just on clergymen already ordained and beneficed, but on young men about to embark on a clerical career. By the 1840s many unsuspecting incumbents found themselves with curates imbued with Tractarian ideals at university. The more perceptive critics were quick to recognise the danger but by that time much of the damage had been done.

Two other important projects developed out of the *Tracts for the Times*. These were the *Library of the Fathers*, launched by Pusey's edition of St Augustine's *Confessions* in 1838, and the *Library of Anglo-Catholic Theology*, in which 88 volumes of the works of post-Reformation high church divines were reprinted and edited between 1841 and 1863. In 1844 William Maskell, chaplain to Bishop Phillpotts of Exeter, published *The Ancient Liturgy of the Church of England*, to be followed two years later by his *Monumenta Ritualia Ecclesiae Anglicanae*, the two volumes being significant contributions to the revival of liturgical studies in the Church of England, which reached its peak in the last quarter of the nineteenth and the first quarter of the twentieth centuries with the work of Walter Howard Frere, bishop of Truro, and the publications of the Alcuin Club and the Henry Bradshaw Society.

Ecclesiology

For the first few years of its existence the impact of the Oxford Movement on the Church of England was entirely theological, and its area of operation almost exclusively academic. Had the movement remained thus limited in its outlook it is likely that its impact would have been very short-lived. One of the principal means of extending the popular influence of Tractarian teaching was provided by the establishment of the Cambridge Camden Society founded in 1839 by John Mason Neale[13] and Benjamin Webb[14]. The principal aim of the Cambridge Camden Society was to promote the restoration of existing churches, the building of new ones, and the furnishing of both according to its own interpretation of what was correct Gothic architecture. An interest in Gothic architecture was not new, nor was it confined to Britain. Throughout Northern Europe architects had been designing in Gothic from the beginning of the century. In Britain churches had been built in a sort of debased Gothic during the late seventeenth and early eighteenth centuries, and after that in a romantic Gothic which was the architectural equivalent of the contemporary Gothic novel. At the same time, however, churches were still being built in the Classical style. The leading exponent of a more correct Gothic style was Augustus Welby Northmore Pugin (1812-1852), an early Anglican convert to Roman Catholicism, who began publishing books on architecture and designing churches and houses in 1835. The Cambridge Camdenians were essentially disciples of Pugin. They were particularly anxious to alter the internal arrangements of most Anglican churches, which had become preaching houses with the pulpit dominant, and cluttered with galleries and pews. They wanted to clear the chancels of pews, have a proper sanctuary with the altar raised on steps and with a proper reredos, a clear view of the altar from the nave with the pulpit and reading pew placed well to the side of the chancel opening, and the font placed at the west end. Later they advocated the introduction of lecterns, choir stalls in the chancel with robed choristers, lighted candles and frontals on the altar, screens, side chapels, organs removed from the west end gallery to an organ chamber off the chancel, sedilia and piscinae, credence tables, representational stained glass, in fact a return, according to their own interpretations, to what English churches might have looked like in the fourteenth century before late medieval corruption had set in

From 1841 until 1868 the Society, which was renamed the Ecclesiological Society in 1846, published a journal, *The Ecclesiologist,* which was caustic but influential. It condemned everything that it considered vulgar, pagan or Protestant. It encouraged Gothicism and gave practical hints on how it could be achieved. From the architectural revolution it was only a small, but dangerous, step to liturgical innovation. At first the leading Tractarians, though they had laid great emphasis on Catholic doctrine, had not really considered its practical implications. By the late 1830s a small group of Tractarians who were parochial incumbents had begun to say, and sometimes even to sing, Morning and Evening Prayer publicly in their churches, and to celebrate, as a separate service at an early hour, on Sundays and Red Letter Saints' Days, the Holy Communion. These parochial incumbents then began to introduce a greater degree of ceremonial into their services: lighted candles and coloured stoles, robed choirs, preaching in a surplice instead of a black gown, bowings and crossings, taking the eastward position in the communion service and mixing water with wine when preparing the chalice. All were intended to bring Anglican liturgical practices into line with traditional Catholic ones, though most were merely revivals of Anglican practices common in the seventeenth century, which in some places had survived until comparatively recently. However, many Evangelicals, broad churchmen and even moderate high churchmen, steeped in a tradition of profound national anti-Catholicism, were quick to condemn these liturgical innovations as romanising. Some, such as Francis Close of Cheltenham, later dean of Carlisle, even condemned church restoration itself as leading to popery, though the strength of the prevailing aesthetic climate ensured that eventually even

Evangelicals and dissenters had to come to terms with the desire for greater decency and symbolism in the design and liturgical arrangement of churches.

Crisis and Secession

Whilst ecclesiology posed difficulties for some conservative high churchmen, difficulties of even greater magnitude were being posed for the more advanced high churchmen, both by hostility to their position and their condemnation as romanisers, and by what they felt to be unfortunate government patronage of broad churchmen with a low church view of the doctrine of the church. Many high churchmen, and some Evangelicals, were outraged by the appointment of R.D. Hampden, a broad churchman who had argued in favour of a pragmatic approach to dogmatic theology, to the Regius professorship of Divinity at Oxford in 1836, and later, in 1847, to the bishopric of Hereford. Many high church consciences were similarly discomforted by the joint participation of Anglicans and Prussian Lutherans in the Jerusalem bishopric established in 1841. The period between 1840 and 1860 was marked by a series of crises in which groups of high churchmen found their position within the Anglican establishment untenable and seceded to the Roman Catholic Church. The secessions were accompanied by considerable publicity and fierce attacks on both the beliefs and the characters of those who had seceded.

The first great crisis in the history of the Oxford Movement followed Hurrell Froude's early death in 1836. Keble and Newman decided to publish his surviving *opera* in four volumes during 1838-9. Most of the *Remains* consisted of extracts from Froude's private diary which contained, in intimate detail, a full account of his ascetic and spiritual practices, his deep feelings of doubt and self-loathing, and his consciousness of his sinfulness, together with strong support for clerical celibacy, devotion to the Blessed Virgin Mary and violent denunciations of the sixteenth-century reformers. The result was catastrophic and one can only be amazed at the naivety of the editors in publishing such material. Statements to the effect that 'the Reformation was a limb badly set; it must be broken again to be righted' caused a storm of protest in a country where anti-Catholicism was a deeply entrenched position brought about by a genuine belief that the papacy was daily waiting for an opportunity to reclaim the English church and liquidate its opponents. There ensued a deliberately calculated scheme to embarrass the Tractarians by organising an appeal to erect a suitable memorial in Oxford to the Protestant martyrs of the English Reformation. Tractarians were to be placed in the awkward position of having either to subscribe to an object which was really an attack on themselves or else publicly to suggest that they agreed with Froude's opinions on the Reformers and were thus disloyal to the national church. Only a few, including Newman, felt brave enough to take the latter course, and his iniquity was compounded in the eyes of his critics with the publication of the defiantly pro-Roman *Tract XC* in 1841. The tract was immediately condemned by the heads of most Oxford Colleges and at the request of the bishop of Oxford Newman agreed that the series should be suspended. Shortly afterwards he retired to Littlemore where he had established a chapel-of-ease to the parish church of St Mary's, Oxford, of which he had been the vicar since 1828, and contemplated his future position. He was to resign this living in 1843, and became a Roman Catholic two years later.

In 1843 E.B. Pusey preached before the University of Oxford a sermon on 'The Holy Eucharist a Comfort to the Penitent', in which he strongly defended the doctrine of the Real Presence which had been held in some form by most high churchmen, but which was repugnant to Evangelicals and broad churchmen. He was immediately condemned by his professorial colleagues and suspended from preaching for two years. Many of those who had disregarded the Oxford Movement in the 1830s began to fear that if the Movement was allowed to prosper, it could transform the Church of England and possibly even lead to reunion with Rome, and they were determined to bring it down. In 1844 two of the more extreme Tractarians, Frederick William Faber[15] and William George Ward[16], played into the critics' hands with, respectively, an openly pro-Roman Catholic *Life of St Wilfrid,* the protagonist of the Romans claims at the Synod of Whitby, and *The Ideal of a Christian Church,* which was clearly not the reformed Church of England. In fact Ward went so far as to allege that he personally accepted all Roman Catholic doctrine as an Anglican but had received no ecclesiastical censure. Thus challenged the heads of the

Oxford Colleges determined to call Ward's bluff. They summoned a special meeting of Convocation, at which all holding master's or doctor's degrees were entitled to vote, to censure Ward's book, to degrade him from his degrees, and to condemn, retrospectively, *Tract XC*. The Convocation was held on 13 February 1845 and attracted an enormous attendance from all over the country, from bishops and members of Parliament down to obscure country clergymen. Ward defended his book but it was finally condemned by 777 votes to 386. The proposal to degrade him from his degrees, which some considered unnecessarily petulant, was only carried by 569 votes to 511. Before, however, a vote could be taken on *Tract XC*, the two proctors, of whom one was Richard William Church[17], the future historian of the Oxford Movement, uttered the fatal words "nobis procuratoribus non placet". The third proposal, which might well also have been carried, was vetoed by the desire of one of Newman's disciples not to see the acknowledged leader of the movement unnecessarily humiliated.

It was not enough. Newman had ceased to be active, and had been wrestling with his conscience since at least 1841. In 1845 Newman, Faber and Ward all seceded to Rome taking with them a significant number of the more extreme Tractarians. The leadership of the movement passed to Pusey. The crisis of 1845 was regarded at the time as a great watershed, and continued to be so regarded by many of the movement's early historians. In fact it was only one of a series of crises that the movement passed through after the publication of Froude's *Remains,* and with each new crisis there was at least a trickle, and sometimes more like a flood, of secessions. They were actively encouraged by the sympathetic attitude of some Roman Catholic leaders, especially the future Cardinal Nicholas Wiseman. Those converts who were unmarried were rushed through the formalities of Roman Catholic ordination training. Some later became the most aggressive and ultramontane protagonists of the Roman Catholic and papal claims. Others, particularly Newman, found themselves as isolated in their new spiritual home as they had been in the Church of England.

Another major batch of secessions occurred in the early 1850s as a result of the Gorham Judgement. The Tractarians' only openly episcopal supporter, Bishop Phillpotts of Exeter, refused to institute an Evangelical, the Revd. G.C. Gorham, to the vicarage of Brampford Speke in his diocese on the grounds that he denied the doctrine of baptismal regeneration as taught historically by the Church of England in common with the Roman Catholic and Eastern Orthodox churches. For most Evangelicals infant baptism was a rather meaningless symbol; the real test of true Christianity was the conversion experience. A very complicated lawsuit followed with Gorham eventually appealing to the Judicial Committee of the Privy Council, a court of appeal established in 1833 which, among other things, had taken over the ecclesiastical jurisdiction of the High Court of Delegates established by Henry VIII after the abolition of appeals to Rome. The Judicial Committee attempted to fudge the issues by attributing to Gorham a view of baptism which he did not actually hold and then declaring that view to be 'not contrary or repugnant to the doctrine of the Church of England'. The Bishop of Exeter, however, still refused to institute Gorham, and in the end the institution had to be carried out by the Evangelical Archbishop of Canterbury, J.B. Sumner. What angered high churchmen most was not the actual judgement but the fact that a secular and not an ecclesiastical court had made the final decision in what was a doctrinal dispute. Their confidence in the Court's judgement was further shaken by the fact that one of the lay judges and the bishop of London, C.J. Blomfield, neither of whom were high churchmen, had dissented from the judgement. Among the many secessions caused by the Gorham Judgement were those of archdeacons Manning and Wilberforce. The contempt with which the Judicial Committee was regarded by high churchmen was of considerable significance in the 1850s and 1860s when attempts were made to prosecute high churchmen for heretical doctrine and illegal liturgical practices.

Retrospect:
The Significance of 1845

It has been suggested earlier that the significance of Newman's secession to Rome in 1845 may have been overestimated, and it is perhaps appropriate at this point to consider this matter in more detail. Some past work on the Oxford Movement, including Dean Church's pioneering study, has indeed regarded the movement proper as only covering the thirteen years between 1833 and 1845, and anything happening thereafter as essentially peripheral. There are two particular issues here. One is the role of Newman in the Oxford Movement. The other is the relationship between Tractarianism and later Anglo-Catholicism.

The position occupied by Newman in the events of the 1830s and 1840s is to a large extent distorted by his intellectual stature. There is no doubt that in terms of original thinking Newman stood head and shoulders above virtually everybody else within both Anglicanism and Roman Catholicism in the nineteenth century. It is for this reason that his position both as an Anglican and as a Roman Catholic was a fairly uneasy one. It would certainly be a mistake to regard Newman as representing the main strand of the Oxford Movement, though in the 1830s he was the movement's most prolific and most influential writer, and he personally attracted a whole group of disciples, many of whom followed him to Rome. Keble, Pusey and Froude more truly represented the various main trends within the Oxford Movement than did Newman: Keble, moderate, traditional, careful, unadventurous high churchmanship; Pusey, a more positive though not extreme variety of high churchmanship, which was perhaps the nearest to what can be regarded as mainstream Tractarianism; Froude, the more extreme high church position of the type later represented by the advanced ritualists. Newman, it must be remembered, had begun to withdraw from the active leadership of the movement even before the publication of *Tract XC*, and his withdrawal was virtually complete thereafter. He was also a convert from Evangelicalism and he had consciously developed his religious position between 1820 and 1840; Keble on the other hand appears not really to have developed at all and maintained much the same religious position in the 1860s as he had in the 1820s. Newman's eventual secession to Rome in 1845 may have been a profound psychological blow, but it was certainly not unexpected and it is doubtful if it had more than a temporary dispiriting effect on the other Tractarians. It is, however, true that it was interpreted as being cataclysmic by many contemporary commentators, who overestimated Newman's 'leadership' of the Oxford Movement.

The relationship between the early Tractarians and the later Anglo-Catholics has also been misinterpreted by those who have seen 1845 as the end of a particular series of events, rather than just one event in a religious movement which had begun much earlier and continued much later. A number of historians of the Oxford Movement, mostly Anglicans, have tried to suggest that there was a fundamental difference between the doctrinal position of the early Tractarians, and the later beliefs and practices of ritualists which they have generally regarded as excessive and non-Anglican. There is absolutely no evidence to support this theory. Liturgical experiment, however advanced, was the logical outcome of Tractarian teaching. The early Tractarians included among their number men like Froude who were already very pro-Roman Catholic in their theology. Many other Tractarians, like Pusey, who may initially have regarded liturgical experiment as peripheral to their own interests, ended up either as practising ritualists themselves, or at the very least as defenders of ritualistic practices. It is true that as it progressed the Oxford Movement lost some of its earlier supporters, but these were on the whole the more moderate high churchmen who failed to appreciate that Tractarian teaching in the religious and political climate of the 1830s was likely to lead to more than just a revival of the traditional high churchmanship of previous years. What the Oxford Movement did more than anything else, partially by design, partially by accident, was to restore among the clergy and some lay members of the Church of England a confidence in the church as a divine institution, capable of independent action, of reforming its own abuses, defining its own theology and organising its own liturgy. It was in this context that aggressive high churchmanship was likely to develop in the way that it did, and there is plenty of indication in early Tractarian writing that even some of the more cautious high churchmen were fully aware of these implications. To end the history of the Oxford Movement in 1845 is as meaningless as to end that of political reform in 1832.

The Growth of Ritualism

The Tractarian Parish

Readers of *Dr Thorne* will be aware of Trollope's description of the Revd. Caleb Oriel (note the surname), the new Tractarian rector of Greshamsbury:

> "Mr Oriel was a man of family and fortune, who, having gone to Oxford with the usual views of such men, had become inoculated there with very High-Church principles, and had gone into orders influenced by a feeling of enthusiastic love for the priesthood ... He delighted in lecterns and credence-tables, in services at dark hours of winter mornings when no one would attend, in high waistcoats and narrow white neckties, in chanted services and intoned prayers, and in all the paraphernalia of Anglican formalities which have given such offence to those of our brethren who live in daily fear of the scarlet lady ... He eschewed matrimony, imagining that it became him as a priest to do so; he fasted rigorously on Fridays; and the neighbours declared that he scourged himself."

Dr Thorne was published in 1858, and by that date most parts of England and Wales could boast at least one clergyman of the same type as Mr Oriel. In London there were Tractarian ministries at the Margaret Chapel under Frederick Oakley[18] from 1839, and at St Paul's, Knightsbridge, under William James Early Bennett[19] from 1840. Leeds was another important urban base for early Tractarian parochial activity with three high churches in the 1840s. William John Butler[20] and Thomas Thellusson Carter[21] had made their respective Berkshire parishes important centres of Tractarian activity before 1850. Many other English and Welsh parishes, both urban and rural, had known at least one Tractarian incumbent before the end of the century.

Tractarian incumbents, however, could not expect promotion until towards the end of the nineteenth century, and even then the known hostility of Queen Victoria had to be skilfully overcome. The first English Tractarian bishop, Walter Kerr Hamilton[22], nominated to Salisbury in 1854, owed his preferment to the fact that neither the queen nor the government realised that Hamilton was anything more than the conservative high churchman that his predecessor had been, or that many of his episcopal colleagues were.

Outside England and Wales the influence of the Oxford Movement was quickly felt. In Scotland the Scottish Episcopal Church, which had been traditionally high church since its eclipse by Presbyterianism in the late seventeenth century, was strongly influenced by Tractarianism, though its first Tractarian bishop, Alexander Penrose Forbes[23], was prosecuted for heresy for his defence of the doctrine of the Real Presence in the Eucharist. In Ireland and the Isle of Man, traditional high churchmanship was countered by strong anti-Roman Catholicism, and Tractarian activity was limited to a few churches in Dublin and one church in Douglas. In the traditionally Protestant Channel Islands, however, there were a number of Tractarian parishes by the 1890s. There were also vigorous Tractarian chaplaincies in Europe, to cater for the high church Englishman abroad, notably St Mark's, Florence, and St George's, Paris.

Just as Anglicanism had been exported to the United States and throughout the British Empire, as part of the framework of colonialism, so Tractarianism too found its way around the world. In the United States the growing influence of Tractarians led to considerable conflict within the Protestant Episcopal Church. The Universities' Mission to Central Africa was established as a Tractarian venture in 1857 and eventually led to the creation of five dioceses in East Africa in which Anglo-Catholicism was the only variety of Anglicanism available. In other parts of Africa, India, Australia, New Zealand, and the West Indies, Anglo-Catholicism did not have the monopoly it enjoyed in East Africa but it was certainly well represented.

In some aspects of their parochial ministry Tractarian incumbents did not differ noticeably from their Evangelical predecessors and contemporaries. Both placed a strong emphasis on pastoral visiting, more frequent services, experimental forms of worship, and parochial organisations, particularly those of a social character. Tractarians differed from Evangelicals in their emphasis on the ceremonial aspects of worship, in their pastoral counselling and in their attitude towards social concern. Most Tractarians eschewed the emotionalism of the Evangelical conversion experience, though there were a few, sometimes misleadingly termed Catholic Evangelicals, who tried to combine emotionalism with ceremonial. Tractarian ceremonial developed only slowly. In the 1840s it was restricted largely to intoning the services, having lighted candles on the altar and preaching in the surplice, but even these limited innovations were regarded as popish and were enough to cause riots in Exeter in 1845 and 1848, at East Grinstead between 1848 and 1857, at St Barnabas', Pimlico, in 1850-1 and another London church, St George's-in-the-East, in 1859-60. In other parts of the country, however, the innovations were quietly accepted and greatly extended. Some clergy went out of their way to proceed cautiously, beginning with doctrinal teaching and only proceeding to greater ceremonial when they were sure it would be accepted. By the 1860s advanced Anglo-Catholic churches could be recognised by whether or not they observed what were known as the 'six points': taking the eastward position at the Eucharist; wearing the full eucharistic vestments; mixing water with wine in the chalice; using lighted candles on the altar; using unleavened or wafer bread in the Eucharist; and using incense during the service. Full directions for supplementing the liturgy of the Book of Common Prayer with the ceremonial of the western Catholic church were given in the *Directorium Anglicanum,* the first edition of which was published in 1858.

The principal innovation that the Tractarians brought to pastoral counselling was their encouragement of their parishioners to make a private confession of their sins to a priest and to be sacramentally absolved. Although there is evidence that this practice, certainly encouraged by the high church divines of the seventeenth century, had not entirely died out in the intervening period, its revival by the Tractarians, who nearly all placed great emphasis on it, was very unpopular among English Protestants, who regarded the whole concept as at best indelicate and at worst obscene. Newman, Keble, Pusey, Manning and most of the early leaders of the Oxford Movement all heard confessions, and there were early confessional scandals, alleging the improper questioning of female penitents by young celibate priests, at St Saviour's, Leeds, in 1850 and at All Saints', Maidenhead, in 1858. Attempts to improve confessional technique, through the licensing of confessors, and the publication of a confessors' manual, *The Priest in Absolution*, likewise provoked howls of Protestant outrage. Confession, however, continued to remain an essential part of the Tractarian parochial programme, and individual priests regarded it as the best method of developing within their parishioners an understanding of spirituality. Despite this, however, it remained unpopular with the laity, and even in Tractarian parishes only a small proportion of the congregation were penitents.

In their attitude to social concern Tractarian parish priests saw some forms of social action as important in their own rights, and not simply as a means of converting the irreligious. A number of clergymen in working class districts, such as Charles Fuge Lowder[24], Alexander Heriot Mackonochie[25], Arthur Henry Stanton[26], and Robert William Radcliffe Dolling[27], established very considerable reputations for their social work in deprived communities, and it was Anglo-Catholics who were prominent in the later phases of Christian Socialism in the last quarter of the nineteenth century. It must not however be thought, as has sometimes been implied, that Anglo-Catholics had a monopoly in this field. There were notable Evangelical and moderate Anglicans who made equally significant contributions. Nor should it be thought, as has also sometimes been implied, that Anglo-Catholic parochial activity was increasingly concentrated in working-class parishes. There were many middle-class Anglo-Catholic parishes in urban areas, particularly in the fashionable seaside towns like Brighton, Eastbourne, Folkestone and Scarborough, and many rural Anglo-Catholic parishes, particularly in the West Country and in Yorkshire, where the influence of Tractarian landed families was strong. This influence, in particular, cannot be too strongly emphasised. Many upper-class families were among the staunchest supporters of the Oxford Movement, and many Tractarian clergymen were drawn from their ranks often serving unpaid curacies in working class districts and diverting their own wealth into the building of churches, schools, orphanages, penitentiaries (refuges for prostitutes), social clubs and soup kitchens. Tractarian incumbents owed their livings to Tractarian patrons, at a time when public opinion was very much against them. It is not insignificant for the progress of the Oxford Movement that two out of four prime ministers between 1868 and 1902, William Ewart Gladstone and the Marquess of Salisbury, who between them were prime ministers for all but seven of those years, were themselves disciples of the movement and prepared to support it publicly.

The Religious Life

The social work in many Tractarian parishes was much encouraged by the revival of the religious life for men and women within the Church of England, which was one of the earliest fruits of the Oxford Movement. Indeed a number of high churchmen in the 1830s had argued that such a revival was essential if the religious needs of the urban poor were to be met, since the clergy themselves could not do this alone. Informal attempts to set up quasi-monastic communities were made by Newman at Littlemore and Faber at Elton before they seceded to Rome in 1845. In 1863 Joseph Leycester Lyne[28], popularly known as Father Ignatius, founded his own esoteric community of Anglican Benedictines, to be followed by the very much more stable Society of St John the Evangelist, the Cowley Fathers, founded by Richard Meaux Benson[29] in 1865. Both Father Ignatius and the Cowley Fathers were much in demand for parochial missions which became a feature of high church parishes from the 1860s. No other communities for men were founded, however, until the 1890s. Between 1845 and 1900 no fewer than sixty communities for women were established and only a small proportion of them failed to prosper. Among the first communities established were ones founded by W.J. Butler in his parish of Wantage in 1848, by T.T. Carter in his parish of Clewer in 1851, and by J.M. Neale at East Grinstead in 1855. In 1848 Priscilla Lydia Sellon[30] was persuaded by Bishop Phillpotts of Exeter to set up a community to work among the prostitutes and destitute members of society in Plymouth and Devonport. Within two years she had established an orphanage, a college for sailor boys, a refuge for prostitutes, a home for old sailors and their wives, an industrial school, six lodging houses for poor families, a soup kitchen and five ragged schools. Her sisters were prominent in nursing the victims of cholera epidemics in 1849 and 1853, and during the Crimean War eight sisters were sent out to assist Florence Nightingale in the nursing of wounded soldiers.

Despite their social and educational work Anglican religious communities, particularly those for women, were singled out for the same sort of hysterical attacks as priests who were well-known as confessors, and demands were made in Parliament and in the press for government inspection of convents. People believed that advantage was being taken of rich single women by convent superiors and these beliefs were much strengthened by the revelations of two of Mother Lydia's former nuns, Margaret Goodman and Margaret Cusack. The former published *Experiences of an English Sister of Mercy* in 1862 and *Sisterhoods in the Church of England* in 1863, the latter *Five Years in A Protestant Sisterhood and Ten Years in a Catholic Convent* in 1869. Both revealed disciplinary practices and physical deprivations that the English public found totally unacceptable. There is no doubt that life in some religious houses was austere and the superiors, particularly Mother Lydia and Father Ignatius, unnecessarily dictatorial. As in the case of Anglican priests hearing confessions, part of the problem was inexperience. There were no precedents and Anglican religious superiors had to make things up as they went along, though there was some limited and superficial contact with Roman Catholic religious houses, usually on the continent of Europe. In the end it was found possible to establish sound religious communities for both men and women, but the process was a difficult and painful one, and several communities perished within a few years of their foundation.

Defence and Prosecution

There is no doubt that at the beginning of the Oxford Movement many of its critics were unaware of its likely impact. But the movement caught the imaginations of many of those who had become outraged by the feeling that the Church of England was under constant attack from Whig politicians, dissenters and rationalist free-thinkers. Whilst the critics still thought that this new manifestation of high churchism was a brief passing wonder their criticism had been fairly restrained. But the continued progress and growing extremism of the movement, despite the crises and secessions of the 1840s, convinced the critics that action must be taken. The anti-Roman Catholic frenzy unleashed by the re-establishment of the Roman Catholic hierarchy in 1850, and Wiseman's unfortunately flamboyant attitude towards the whole event, soon fuelled an attack on the Romanists in the Church of England. In 1854 suits were brought in the ecclesiastical courts against Archdeacon George Anthony Denison[31] and the Hon Robert Liddell, vicar of St Paul's, Knightsbridge. The suit against Denison was on the grounds of two sermons preached in Wells Cathedral in which he had defended the doctrine of the Real Presence in the Eucharist, the same grounds on which Pusey had been suspended from preaching in the University of Oxford a decade earlier. Denison, who was among the more aggressive Tractarians and positively encouraged the prosecution, was rather disappointed when his original sentence of deprivation was set aside for technical reasons on appeal. Liddell was prosecuted for alleged liturgical illegalities including the use of an altar cross and candles, coloured frontals and a credence table. He was also upheld on appeal on the grounds that these ornaments were consistent with a rubric in the Prayer Book which ordered that the ornaments of the Church and its ministers should be those in use 'by the authority of Parliament in the second year of the reign of King Edward VI'. High churchmen latched on to this and many later ritual prosecutions were fought over the precise meaning and standing of this imprecise phrase.

The attack on the ritualists through the courts led to the formation of various societies to support the ritualist cause. The earliest was the Society of the Holy Cross established in 1855, followed by the English Church Union in 1859-60. In 1865 the Church Association was formed by extreme Evangelicals to protest against romanising in the Church of England, and it was not long before the Association and the Union were locked into a battle over ritual, the Association instigating prosecutions and the Union seeking to defend those under attack. Prosecutions against Mackonochie at St Alban's, Holborn, and John Purchas at St James', Brighton, eventually resulted in four of the 'six points' (vestments, eastward position, wafer bread and mixed chalice) being ruled illegal. A Royal Commission on Ritual produced a report which was highly critical of liturgical innovation. Archibald Campbell Tait, Archbishop of Canterbury from 1868 until 1882, who had publicly protested against *Tract XC* in 1841, was determined to prevent the spread of ritualism. With the defeat of Gladstone's government in the general election of 1874, he was able to persuade the new prime minister, Disraeli, that legislation was needed. A strong response to ritualism was also favoured by Queen Victoria whose view of religion was rather more in tune with Hanoverian erastianism than the ecclesiastical reforms encouraged by both Evangelicals and Tractarians.

The Public Worship Regulation Act passed by the strongly anti-Tractarian majorities in both houses of Parliament was a deliberate attempt to put down ritualism, 'the mass in masquerade' as Disraeli was to term it. It was opposed by Gladstone and the Marquess of Salisbury and the few other Tractarians in both the Conservative and Liberal parties, but most Liberals voted with the government. The legislation did not have the unqualified support of the bishops. Although all of them publicly made statements condemning excessive ritualism, privately many of the high church bishops were sympathetic and did their best to resist what was being proposed. It was largely as a result of their pressure that a clause was introduced to allow a diocesan bishop to veto a prosecution under the Act, a clause which led eventually to the legislation becoming inoperative. With the passing of the Act the Church Association immediately began a new series of ritual prosecutions. Most of the ritualist clergy decided to refuse to accept the validity of the new court set up under the Act. Only C.J. Ridsdale, vicar of St Peter's, Folkestone, accepted a judgement against him on the use of vestments, and asked Archbishop Tait for a dispensation from the proper observance of the Ornaments Rubric, to which Tait graciously consented. Five ritualist priests, two in London and one each in Birmingham, Liverpool and Manchester, were imprisoned for short periods for failing to obey the judgements of the new courts. Public opinion, which had strongly supported the Act, was not prepared to support the ultimate consequence of defiance. Although many more prosecutions were started they were vetoed by most bishops, including some Evangelicals. Only J.C. Ryle, bishop of Liverpool from 1880 until 1900, was not prepared to compromise. The Act had completely failed in its objectives. As a result there was an enormous upsurge in ritual innovations in Anglican churches. The number of churches in which vestments were used increased from 336 in 1882 to 2,158 in 1901, and the number in which incense was used from 9 to 393 in the same period.

The Church Association tried a new tactic. In 1888 it engineered the prosecution of the most extreme of the high church bishops, Edward King[32], for alleged illegalities in ceremonial, but that too failed. Tait's successor as Archbishop of Canterbury, the moderate high church E.W. Benson, sitting with five episcopal assessors, found in favour of the bishop on most points, in a judgement delivered in 1890. Extreme Protestant frustration found its outlet in the Protestant Truth Society, founded in the same year by John Kensit. Kensit and his supporters demonstrated at most of the well-known ritualist churches and at the enthronement ceremonies of high church bishops, and Kensit himself contested Brighton as an Independent Conservative, on an anti-ritualist platform, in 1900. Although he was not elected he polled a respectable vote in a town which had become notorious for the number and extremism of its ritualist churches.

The debate over minute questions of ritual and vesture strikes the modern mind as unbelievably trivial, and in a sense it was. But the issues that divided the church and public opinion were symbolic of a greater division over matters of strong religious principle. Those who were prepared to go to prison rather than give up the use of vestments or incense felt themselves to be defending much more than mere matters of ceremonial. They felt themselves to be defending the right of the Church of England to be part of the one, holy, Catholic and apostolic church, against those who wanted to turn it into a Protestant sect. They felt themselves to be defending the independence of the church and its clergy to make its own decisions in matters of religious doctrine and practice, against those who wanted the church to be controlled by Parliament as the sovereign body of the nation. Similarly those who sought to restrict these freedoms, or churchmen who felt that some sort of brake should be applied to ritualist experimentation, were also defending what they regarded as matters of important political or religious principle: a reformed church purged of Roman corruption or the maintenance of the balanced position of the Church of England as the *via media* between the extreme viewpoints of non-episcopal Protestantism and ultramontantist Roman Catholicism.

Prayer Book Revision

It was quite clear by the end of the nineteenth century that the attempt to apply any sort of brake to Anglican high churchmanship, whether by religious or by political means, had failed. The bishops were hamstrung by private patronage and clerical security of tenure. Only unbeneficed curates could be effectively disciplined, and even they could not be prevented from obtaining livings. Constitutional methods of restraint had given way to crude, direct action. The failure to prevent the growth of ritualism could be put down to the simple fact that support for the Oxford Movement in some areas was too strong. There is no doubt that some of the moderate high church bishops were totally ambivalent in their attitudes. What they might say publicly to reassure the critics was not followed up by any real action, and the Evangelical polemicists were not far wrong when they asserted that many bishops had secretly encouraged and promoted ritualism. They had certainly allowed it to take root. The ritualist lobby had powerful support too in the sympathies of Gladstone and the Marquess of Salisbury, and of the many landed families who as patrons of livings deliberately appointed known ritualists to livings within their gift. Many ritualist parish clergy had built up large and loyal congregations. Determined ritualist priests knew that if they were prepared to face the unpleasantness of a long struggle with their opponents they would eventually be able to carry their point and even turn public hostility into public sympathy.

It was against this background that Parliament set up a Royal Commission on Ecclesiastical Discipline in 1904. The minutes of the Commission contain detailed evidence of

Anglo-Catholic practices in more than five hundred churches in England and Wales. The Commission reported two years later and concluded both that ecclesiastical discipline in liturgical matters had completely broken down and that the existing limitations on ritual practice were too severe. They recommended that liturgical practices which had become widespread within the Church of England, such as all the 'six points' with the exception of incense, should probably be declared lawful, but that strong action should be taken to restrain the more extreme Anglo-Catholic practices.

It is difficult to appreciate how far some Anglo-Catholics had gone. There had always been differences between the pro- and anti-Romanists. By the last quarter of the nineteenth century a clear rift had developed between those Anglo-Catholics whose liturgical vision was a restoration of medievalist ceremonial, and those who condemned this approach as ludicrously antiquarian, and advocated instead the adoption of modern Roman Catholic ceremonial. The ideals of the former school were propounded by the Alcuin Club, founded in 1897 'to encourage and assist in the practical study of ceremonial, and the arrangement of churches, their furniture and ornaments, in accordance with the rubrics of the Book of Common Prayer'. Medievalist ceremonial was popularised by Percy Dearmer[33], who published his *Parson's Handbook* in 1899. Roman Catholic ceremonial was propounded in the rival *Ritual Notes*, and in the late 1870s Frederick George Lee[34] went so far as to set up an Order of Corporate Reunion to facilitate the eventual submission of the Church of England to the Holy See. A few extremist Anglican churches abandoned the prayer book altogether, and at one London church by the early twentieth century all the services were said or sung in Latin. It was this type of extremism that most Anglicans were anxious to suppress. The immediate outcome of the Royal Commission's report was the setting-up of the mechanism for revising the Book of Common Prayer, a process which was to take twenty years. In the intervening period there was a further advance in ritualism, much of which took place during the 1914-18 war. The huge numbers of bereavements popularised the high church practice of praying for the departed. The need to make proper provision for sick communion led to a substantial rise in the number of churches in which the Blessed Sacrament was perpetually reserved. When, after much lobbying from both high church and Evangelical pressure groups, the final version of the new Prayer Book appeared, it made substantial concessions to high churchmen on the questions of ornaments and vestments, on reservation, on prayer for the departed, and on the addition of various widely used prayers, such as the *Benedictus* and *Agnus Dei* in the communion service. The revised book did not go far enough for advanced high churchmen but was much disliked by the Evangelicals. Although it was made clear that the revised book was meant to be an alternative to, and not a substitute for, the Prayer Book of 1662, it was Evangelical lobbying which ensured its eventual defeat when it was brought before Parliament in 1927. A rather less high church revision was then brought back to Parliament in 1928, and although this was even less acceptable to high churchmen it was still too high church to satisfy the Evangelicals, and once again it was defeated. The debate over the revised Prayer Book provoked another series of Evangelical attacks on ritualism, and a number of emotional high church demonstrations in the form of local and national Anglo-Catholic Congresses between 1920 and 1933. With the defeat of the revised Prayer Book, however, it became very difficult for diocesan bishops to lay down the limits of liturgical practice, though a number tried to do so. It was only as a result of the Parish Communion movement in the years after 1945 that a consensus eventually emerged on liturgical reform and new experimental services were officially ratified. With this new consensus much of the old emnity between Anglo-Catholics and Evangelicals eventually disappeared, and in recent years the two extremes have frequently joined forces against what they regard as a common enemy, the theological liberalism propounded by the modern successors of the old broad churchmen.

The Oxford Movement in Perspective

Victorian Theology

The older partisan histories of the Oxford Movement frequently gave the impression that all the reforms in the Victorian Church of England, all the spiritual leadership in working-class parishes, all the theological and liturgical scholarship of the nineteenth century, was somehow a Tractarian monopoly. This is of course absolute nonsense. In terms of theological scholarship most disciples of the Oxford Movement were diehard Conservatives. Even Pusey, who had been moderately sympathetic to German biblical criticism in the 1820s, developed a systematic theology based rigidly on the early fathers, the medieval philosophers and the high church Anglican divines of the seventeenth century. When the English biblical debate opened in the 1860s the Tractarians were fundamentalists almost to a man. It was only towards the end of the nineteenth century that a liberal Anglo-Catholic school of theology emerged with the publication of *Lex Mundi* in 1889. Most of the older Tractarians, including their leading theologian and faithful disciple of Pusey, Henry Parry Liddon[35], were deeply shocked and were loud in the condemnation of any deviation from traditional opinions on the inspiration of the scriptures. The leaders of the new school of liberal Anglo-Catholicism included Charles Gore[36], Henry Scott Holland[37], Robert Campbell Moberly[38], Francis Paget[39] and Edward Stuart Talbot[40], all of whom contributed to *Lux Mundi,* and three of whom later became bishops. Gore and Talbot were, respectively, the first principal of Pusey House and first warden of Keble College, the two institutions founded in Oxford in memory of the two early leaders of the Oxford Movement.

The Publication of *Lux Mundi* was a theological watershed. It demonstrated that the third generation of

Tractarians, or at least some of them, were capable of breaking loose from the theological conservatism in which the Oxford Movement had been conceived. Its approach was paralleled by the modernist movement within Roman Catholicism, though this movement was effectively crushed in its infancy by the power of a conservative papacy. Liberal Anglo-Catholicism had a longer life and found much respect in Anglican theological circles. It found rather less respect among the more extreme Anglo-Catholic clergy who thought like Liddon, and Gore, Paget and Talbot found themselves much distrusted as bishops by those who in theory should have welcomed such high church appointments.

Outside the realms of strictly academic theology one should note the role of the Tractarians in the provision of theological training for the clergy. Of the early theological colleges, Chichester (1839), Wells (1840), Cuddesdon (1854) and Salisbury (1860), were all founded on very definite high church principles. In the area of popular theology one should note the considerable Tractarian contribution in the field of hymnology. The two major Anglican hymnals still in use in most cathedrals and parish churches, *Hymns Ancient and Modern,* first published in 1861, and *The English Hymnal*, launched in 1906, were both high church compilations, though the former eventually came to be regarded as a mainstream Anglican document, given the ultimate accolade of respectability by its use among the armed forces. Hymns by Faber, Keble and Newman came to be among the most popular of those sung in churches, whilst the work of J.M. Neale, who translated a large number of hymns from both Greek and Latin texts, as well as writing new ones, was particularly helpful in popularising medieval religious poetry and thereby enriching the liturgical practices of the Victorian and post-Victorian church.

The Role of the Clergy

The contribution of the Oxford Movement to the liturgical transformation of the Victorian Church of England can hardly be exaggerated. Practices aimed at recovering greater decency and lost ceremonial in public worship, which were confined to a few high churchmen in the 1840s had been adopted by many who would certainly not have described themselves as high churchmen by the end of the century. But even more important than this was the impact that the Oxford Movement had on the traditional role of the clergy within English society. Before 1830 the role of the clergyman within society could perhaps best be described as 'social' rather than 'spiritual'. Within a predominantly agricultural society the parson and the squire were the twin pillars of authority and continuity. They sat together as justices of the peace. They were both landowners. Whilst the parish priest carried out his pastoral and spiritual duties within the confines of contemporary expectations, which were different from those of the nineteenth or twentieth centuries, these were only a part of a wider role. This conception of the role of the clergy was seriously threatened by the growing industrialisation and secularisation of English society after 1750. What the Oxford Movement gave to the clergy was a new concept of their role in society, one which was not primarily social or quasi-political, but one which was profoundly and pre-eminently spiritual. Priesthood was a vocation. The priest was set apart from secular society to provide spiritual leadership to represent man to God, and God to man. There was a return to the medieval concept of the mediatorial role of the priest, which was emphasised particularly in his sacramental function as laid down in the Prayer Book ordinal. He was to forgive the penitent and to celebrate the Eucharist.

This new concept of priestly vocation, which was perhaps the most important legacy of the Oxford Movement, and which goes a long way to explain clerical support for Tractarianism, was given outward expression in new styles of dress and the introduction of high waistcoats, frock coats and stiff collars. The clergy became a profession apart, to be treated with reverence, or suspicion, or even mild contempt, depending on one's religious sympathies. Ritualist clergy, in particular, partly because of their role as confessors, partly also as a result of their preference for celibacy in many cases, became very much detached from secular society, even where they were held in great affection by their parishioners. Making the clergy dress differently from other people, seeing bishops processing in copes and mitres, all added to the isolation. And many clergymen encouraged the trend. The most extreme ritualist clergymen adopted the new Roman Catholic practice of encouraging their congregations to call them 'father'. Evangelical allegations that the laity were becoming priest-ridden were not without foundation, though their own clergy were glad enough to benefit from the new trends.

Ecclesia Anglicana

Perhaps the most important outcome of the Oxford Movement, in both a positive and a negative sense, was its impact, over a long period, on relations between the Church of England and various other Christian denominations both at home and abroad. It would not be unfair to say that the pre-Tractarian church had little contact with religious life outside England. On the positive side the Oxford Movement brought the Church of England once again into limited contact with the Roman Catholic and Eastern Orthodox churches. Some early intitiatives were taken by John Rouse Bloxham[41], Newman's curate at Littlemore, where he introduced various liturgical innovations, who carried on a significant correspondence with the convert Roman Catholic squire, Ambrose Lisle Phillipps (later changing his surname to De Lisle), in the early 1840s. Another fellow of Magdalen, William Palmer (not to be confused with William Palmer of Worcester, mentioned earlier) was at the same time making important contacts with Eastern Orthodox Christians, paying visits to Russia in 1840 and 1842. Arising from these early contacts were the establishment of the Association for the Promotion of the Unity of Christendom in 1857 and the Eastern Churches Association in 1864, the leading light in the former being F.G. Lee and in the latter J.M. Neale.

There were substantial divisions among high churchmen, however, on their attitude to Roman Catholicism. Early on, in the 1830s, high churchmen had developed what was known as the 'branch theory' of Catholic Christendom. The theory held that as a result of the schisms within the church there was no one part of the church which could claim a monopoly of truth, but that all those 'branches' of the church that had maintained the apostolic succession in the episcopate might be counted as 'branches' of the one, holy, catholic and apostolic church. Later this theory was developed to justify the existence of national churches as the true manifestation of

Catholicism within that country. Thus the Roman Catholic church was the true Catholic church of France, Italy, Spain and Portugal, the Orthodox church that of Greece or Russia, the Lutheran church (which had maintained episcopacy) that of Sweden, the Old Catholic (Jansenist) church that of Holland, and the Anglican church that of the British Isles. Although some Anglican high churchmen argued from this premise in favour of close relations with Roman Catholics, some saw the growing presence of Roman Catholicism as an unwelcome intrusion into the British religious scene. If the Anglican church was the Catholic Church of England then all Catholics in England ought to be members of it. The growth of Roman Catholicism swelled by Irish immigration and Anglican secessions, the restoration of the Roman Catholic hierarchy, which seemed to encourage active proselytisation, and the vigorous attacks on high churchmen as crypto-Papists, forced some Tractarians into a defensive anti-Roman Catholic position. For them the Roman Catholic church was to be denounced as the Italian Mission.

Of a very different frame of mind was the second Viscount Halifax, who became President of the English Church Union in 1868, and after Pusey's death the unofficial leader of the high church party. In 1890 he began conversations with Roman Catholic friends on the Continent of Europe aimed at promoting reunion between the Anglican and Roman Catholic churches. The English Roman Catholic leadership, however, had since Wiseman's death been predominantly ultramontanist and consequently very hostile to the Church of England, encouraged by some of the new fanatical converts like Manning and Ward, and as a result of its machinations the conversations were brought to an abrupt halt by the papal bull, *Apostolicae Curae,* of 1896 in which Anglican orders were declared null and void. Halifax, then in his eighties, was to raise the whole issue again in the 1920s, but these discussions also were abortive.

It could, however, be argued that the Oxford Movement had a negative effect on relations between Anglican and Protestant churches. As early as 1841 most high churchmen protested against Anglicans and non-episcopalian Lutherans joining together in the setting up of the Jerusalem bishopric. Thereafter it was high churchmen who encouraged the Church of England to maintain its strong opposition to dissent, which some of the broad churchmen and Evangelicals would have liked to moderate. Attempts to promote unions between Anglicans and other Protestants, particularly abroad, after 1900 were strongly resisted by Anglo-Catholics, and they have been accused of holding back the cause of Christian unity by many of their critics, and of a total lack of reality in their argument that any form of Christain unity which did not involve Roman Catholic and Eastern Orthodox Christians was unacceptable. This debate between high churchmen and others within the Anglican communion has continued to be a significant factor in Anglican relations with Protestant churches, including various reunion schemes in the 1960s and 1970s.

During the nineteenth century, principally as a result of Tractarian theology, the Church of England developed a new consciousness of her unique role among the churches of Christendom. For W.F. Hook, and many other high churchmen, she was the *via media* between the excesses of Rome on the one hand and the wretchedness of dissent on the other. For many Anglicans she later became the vital 'bridge' church which would, by maintaining within herself features of both the Catholic and the Protestant traditions, succeed in uniting these two traditions. Linked with these views there arose a new feeling of religious nationalist pride which identified the Church of England as the upholder of the historic Christian tradition of the British people. The concept of *ecclesia anglicana,* which had been so vibrant in the late medieval period, had been reasserted triumphantly, and in not such a very different guise.

Notes

1. John Keble (1792-1866), fellow of Oriel from 1811, and tutor 1817-23, resigning to assist his father in his country cure in Gloucestershire; elected Professor of Poetry at Oxford in 1831; vicar of Hursley, Hampshire, from 1836.
2. E.B. Pusey (1800-1882), fellow of Oriel from 1823, Regius Professor of Hebrew and canon of Christ Chruch, Oxford, from 1828.
3. J.H. Newman (1801-1890), fellow of Oriel from 1822, vicar of St Mary's, Oxford, 1828-43; seceded to Rome in 1845, established the Birmingham Oratory in 1849, and created Cardinal in 1879.
4. R.H. Froude (1803-1836), fellow of Oriel from 1826 and tutor from 1827.
5. H.J. Rose (1795-1838), vicar of Horsham, Surrey, 1821-30, rector of Hadleigh, Suffolk, 1830-33, Professor of Divinity in the University of Durham, 1833-34, and Principal of King's College, London, from 1836.
6. A.P. Percival (1799-1853), fellow of All Souls College, Oxford, 1821-25, and rector of East Horsley, Surrey, from 1824.
7. William Palmer (1803-1885), fellow of Worcester College, Oxford, from 1831, not to be confused with his namesake, fellow of Magdalen College, Oxford, also a high churchman and expert on the Eastern Orthodox Churches.
8. Charles Marriott (1811-1858), fellow of Oriel College, Oxford, from 1833, first principal of Chichester Theological College, 1839-41, and vicar of St Mary's, Oxford, 1850-55.
9. Isaac Williams (1802-1865), tutor of Trinity College, Oxford, from 1832, and dean from 1833; withdrew from Oxford life and an active part in the Oxford Movement after 1842.
10. W.F. Hook (1798-1875), vicar of Leeds 1837-59, dean of Chichester 1859-75.
11. H.E. Manning (1808-1892), rector of Lavington, Sussex, from 1833, and archdeacon of Chichester from 1841; seceded to Rome in 1851, and succeeded Cardinal Wiseman as archbishop of Westminster in 1865.
12. R.I. Wilberforce (1802-1857), fellow of Oriel College, Oxford, from 1826, and archdeacon of the East Riding from 1841; seceded to Rome in 1854.
13. J.M. Neale (1818-1866), warden of Sackville College, East Grinstead, from 1846.
14. Benjamin Webb (1819-1885), incumbent of St Andrew's, Wells Street, London, from 1862.
15. F.W. Faber (1814-1863), fellow of University College, Oxford, from 1837; rector of Elton, Huntingdonshire, from 1842; seceded to Rome in 1845, established the London Oratory in 1849, devotional writer and hymnologist.
16. W.G. Ward (1812-1882), fellow of Balliol College, Oxford, from 1834; seceded to Rome in 1845.
17. R.W. Church (1815-1890), fellow of Oriel College, Oxford, 1838-52; rector of Whatley, Somerset, 1852-71; dean of St Paul's Cathedral, London, 1871-90.
18. Frederick Oakley (1802-1880), chaplain and fellow of Balliol College, Oxford, from 1827, incumbent of the Margaret Chapel, London, from 1839; seceded to Rome in 1845; canon of the archdiocese of Westminster from 1852.

19 W.J.E. Bennett (1804-1886), incumbent of St Paul's, Knightsbridge, 1840-52, vicar of Frome Selwood, Somerset, from 1852.
20 W.J. Butler (1818-1894), vicar of Wantage 1846-80, canon of Worcester 1880-85, dean of Lincoln 1885-94.
21 T.T. Carter (1808-1901), rector of Clewer from 1844.
22 W.K. Hamilton (1808-1869), vicar of St Peter's-in-the-East, Oxford, 1837-41, canon of Salisbury 1841-54, succeeding Edward Denison as bishop in 1854.
23 A.P. Forbes (1817-1875), briefly vicar of St Saviour's, Leeds in 1847, elected bishop of Brechin in the same year.
24 C.F. Lowder (1820-1880), curate of St Barnabas, Pimlico, 1851-56, and St George's-in-the-East, London, from 1856, establishing the new church and parish of St Peter's, London Docks, between 1860 and 1866.
25 A.H. Mackonochie (1825-1887), curate of Wantage 1852-58 and St George's-in-the-East, London, 1858-62; incumbent of the new church of St Alban's, Holborn, from 1862.
26 A.H. Stanton (1839-1913), curate of St Alban's, Holborn, from 1862, refusing all further preferment.
27 R.W.R. Dolling (1851-1902), missioner of St Agatha, Landport, Portsmouth, 1885-96, and vicar of St Saviour's, Poplar, 1898-1902.
28 J.L. Lyne (1837-1908), curate of St Peter's, Plymouth, from 1860, abbot of Llanthony from 1869.
29 R.M. Benson (1824-1915), vicar of Cowley, Oxford, from 1850.
30 P.L. Sellon (1821-1876), abbess of the combined sisterhood of the Society of the Most Holy Trinity from 1856.
31 G.A. Denison (1805-1896), vicar of East Brent, Somerset, from 1845, and archdeacon of Taunton from 1852.
32 Edward King (1829-1910), curate of Wheatley, Oxfordshire, 1855-58, chaplain 1858-63 and principal 1863-73 of Cuddesdon Theological College, Regius professor of pastoral theology at Oxford, 1873-85, bishop of Lincoln from 1885.
33 Percy Dearmer (1867-1936), vicar of St Mary's, Primrose Hill, Hampstead, 1901-15, professor of ecclesiastical art at King's College, London, 1919-36.
34 F.G. Lee (1832-1902), vicar of All Saints, Lambeth, 1867-99; seceded to Rome in 1901.
35 H.P. Liddon (1829-1890), curate of Wantage 1852-54, vice-principal of Cuddesdon Theological College 1854-59 and St Edmund Hall, Oxford, 1859-62; Dean Ireland professor of exegesis at Oxford and canon of St Paul's Cathedral, London, from 1870.
36 Charles Gore (1853-1932), fellow of Trinity College, Oxford, from 1875 and first principal of Pusey House from 1884; vicar of Radley, Berkshire, 1893-94, canon of Westminster 1894-1902, successively bishop of Worcester 1902-5, Birmingham 1905-11 and Oxford 1911-19; founded the Community of the Resurrection in 1892.
37 H.S. Holland (1847-1918), senior student at Christ Church, Oxford, 1870-84, canon of St Paul's Cathedral, London, 1884-1910, and Regius professor of divinity at Oxford 1910-18.
38 R.C. Moberly (1845-1903), Regius professor of pastoral theology and canon of Christ Church, Oxford, from 1892.
39 Francis Paget (1851-1911), vicar of Bromsgrove, 1882-85, Regius professor of pastoral theology at Oxford 1885-92, dean of Christ Church 1892-1901, and bishop of Oxford 1901-11.
40 E.S. Talbot (1844-1934), first warden of Keble College, Oxford, 1870-89, vicar of Leeds 1889-95, successively bishop of Rochester 1895-1905, Southwark 1905-11, and Winchester 1911-24.
41 J.R. Bloxham (1807-1891), fellow of Magdalen College, Oxford, from 1836, and vicar of Upper Beeding, Sussex, from 1862.

Bibliography

A full and up-to-date bibliography of the Oxford Movement will be found in *Revolution by Tradition: The Catholic Revival in Nineteenth Century Anglicanism*, ed. G. Rowell and P. Cobb, 1983. This guide to further reading is therefore restricted to the most fundamental and easily obtainable secondary studies.

R.W. Church, *The Oxford Movement*, 1891 (reprinted 1970 with introduction by G.F.A. Best).
S.L. Ollard, *A Short History of the Oxford Movement*, 1915 (reprinted 1963 with introduction by A.M. Allchin).
W. Walsh, *Secret History of the Oxford Movement*, 1897 (accurate but exceptionally hostile).
G. Faber, *Oxford Apostles*, 1933 (brilliant but idosyncratic centenary study).
W.O. Chadwick, *The Victorian Church*, 2 vols, 1966-70 (contains best recent summary of the main events).
P.T. Marsh, *The Victorian Church in Decline*, 1969 (contains useful account of early ritualism and the attempts to supress it).
P.F. Anson, *The Call of the Cloister*, 1964 (most comprehensive survey of Anglican monasticism).
J.F. White, *The Cambridge Movement*, 1962 (principal account of the work of the early ecclesiologists).
P.F. Anson, *Fashions in Church Furnishings*, 1965 (wide-ranging study of the developments in ecclesiological taste after 1860).
W.O. Chadwick, *The Mind of the Oxford Movement*, 1960 (useful for the theological background).
D. Bowen, *The Idea of the Victorian Church*, 1968 (contains useful material on ritualist slum parishes).
D. Newsome, *The Parting of Friends*, 1966 (perceptive insight into the discussions among high churchmen in the 1840s).